SUMMER AND WINTER PEOPLE

A Guide to the Pueblos in the Santa Fe Area

SUMMER PEOPLE PEOPLE WINTER PEOPLE

A guide to Pueblos in the Santa Fe Area

Sandra A. Edelman

Sunstone

Santa Fe, New Mexico

Second Revised Edition Copyright © 1986 by Sandra A. Edelman

Printed in the United States of America

10 9 8 7 6 5 4

Library of Congress Cataloging in Publication Data:

Edelman, Sandra A., 1933-
    Summer people, winter people.

    Bibliography: p.
    1. Pueblos--New Mexico--Santa Fe Region--Guide-books.
2. Pueblo Indians--History. 3. Santa Fe Region (N.M.)--
Description and travel--Guide-books. I. Title.
E99.P9E26   1986   917.89'560453   85-22268
ISBN 0-86534-076-5

Published by   SUNSTONE PRESS
                Post Office Box 2321
                Santa Fe, NM 87505-2321 / USA

TABLE OF CONTENTS

Who Are the Pueblo Indians 7
Pueblo History 8
Pueblo Civil Government 10
Pueblo Religion and Society 10
Pueblo Economy 11
An Important Reminder 12
Pueblos North of Santa Fe 12
The Southern and Western Pueblos 17
Bibliography 27
Fiestas, Dances and Ceremonies 29
Index 32

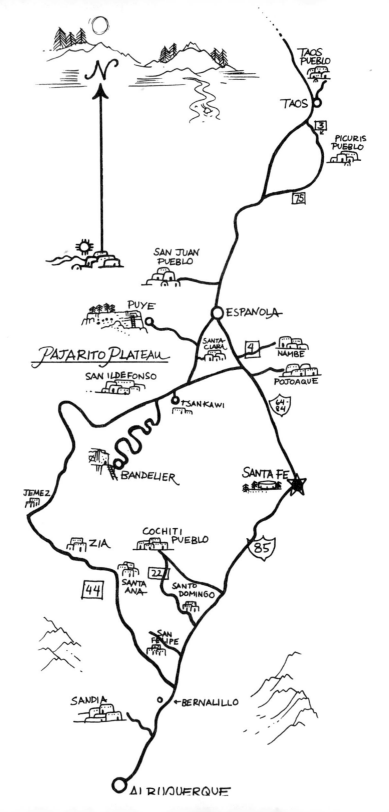

Northern New Mexico is Pueblo country, and if you have not already been to one or more scenic pueblos, it is time to consider what you have missed. The purpose of this Sunstone Guidebook is to provide information which we hope will make your visit to the pueblos as meaningful as it is enjoyable. We hope to answer some of the basic questions about Pueblo Indians: their identity, history and culture in a contemporary and historical perspective.

WHO ARE THE PUEBLO INDIANS?

The simplest definition of the Pueblo Indians is that they are inhabitants of diverse Indian villages who share the same basic historical culture.

Pueblo is a word of Spanish origin meaning village, a name designated by the early Spanish explorers because the Indians lived in compact established villages, similar to the villages of Spain. "Pueblo" may refer to either a person from one of these villages, or to the village itself.

Pueblos are the descendants of the Mogollon (Mo-go-YONE; Spanish Don Juan Ignacio Flores Mogollon, governor of the province of New Mexico, 1712-1715), and the Anasazi (Ahn-ah-SAH-zee; Navajo for "ancient ones"), two prehistoric and long-vanished cultures of the Southwest.

Archaeologists have designated five major periods of development for these people known as Pueblo I – V. The Pueblo I period began approximately in 700 A.D. The Pueblo V period is notable because it coincides with the arrival of the Spanish in 1540, a time when the Pueblos were already well-established and flourishing. The Pueblo V period dates from approximately 1700 to the present.

The scope of this book includes an introduction to each of New Mexico's nineteen pueblos. These are the northern or up-river pueblos:

Nambe	San Juan
Picuris	Santa Clara
Pojoaque	Taos
San Ildefonso	Tesuque

And these are the southern and western pueblos:

Acoma	San Felipe
Cochiti	Santa Ana
Isleta	Santo Domingo
Jemez	Zia
Laguna	Zuni
Sandia	

Each pueblo falls under one of three major linguistic branches: Keresan (Care-es-SAHN); Tanoan (TAH-no-un); and Zunian (ZOON-yee-un). Tanoan consists of three related languages: Tewa (TAY-wah); Towa (TOH-wah); and Tiwa (TEE-wah).

Villages that speak the same languages are:

Tewa — Nambe, Pojoaque, San Ildefonso, San Juan, Santa Clara, Tesuque

Tiwa — Isleta, Picuris, Sandia, Taos

Towa — Jemez

Keresan — Cochiti, Laguna, San Felipe, Santa Ana, Santo Domingo, Zia

Zunian — Zuni

Almost every Pueblo Indian speaks Spanish as a second language; most speak English as well.

PUEBLO HISTORY

In most cases, the pueblos are situated in the same places where the Spanish found them in 1598. And they had been there for hundreds of years before that. Many pueblos have disappeared — no one knows how many, because new ruins are constantly being discovered. Some villages were abandoned more than a thousand years ago because of drought; others were abandoned because a dwindling population made self-sufficiency impossible. A few trace their ancestry to ruin-sites which can be toured by the public today. A good example is San Ildefonso, which is traced back first to Tsankawi (approximately opposite the turn-off to Los Alamos on State Road 4), and before that the cliff dwellings known as Bandelier National Monument. Every Pueblo group has its own "emergence myth" telling how the people first emerged from the earth's womb and how they migrated, over untold centuries, to their present physical and spiritual location. The Tewa, for example, count their migration to the present pueblo in twelve stops; for the San Ildefonsans, Tsankawi and Bandelier were two of those stops.

Archaeology partially reconstructs the prehistory of the Pueblo Indians, but it tells us little more than the development and implications of material culture, migrations, and abandoned villages. It was the arrival of the Spanish which marked the beginning of documented Pueblo history. Doubtless, the first milestone in the record was set in 1680, the year the Pueblos revolted against the Spanish conquerors. Led by Po-pe, a San Juan Indian who served as the spiritual force and organizer of the rebellion, the Pueblos united in a common cause, against heavy odds (arrows versus guns, human feet versus horses) and achieved an almost miraculous victory over their oppressors. The Spanish fled, not to return for twelve years. When they did return, under the leadership of DeVargas, it took them two years to subdue the Indians completely. Not until 1694 was all of "Nuevo Mexico" again in the hands of the Spanish. Twice more the Pueblos attempted to revolt, in 1837 and again in 1847. Neither effort was successful, although in the 1837 plot, Santa Fe was captured, Governor Perez killed (along with several citizens), and a Taos Indian named Jose Gonzalez was elected governor by the dissident group. His administration was brief; shortly after election, Santa Fe was recaptured and Gonzalez executed.

View of the north side of Taos Pueblo

9

Pueblo battles have continued into this century, but for the most part they have taken the modern form of pen and paper.

PUEBLO CIVIL GOVERNMENT

Authority in most pueblos is based on a system begun by the Spanish and continued with only minor changes by the United States government. Usually, civil government is headed by a governor (elected every one or two years; in some Pueblos, however, he is appointed); he is assisted by one or two lieutenant governors ("right-hand man" and "left-hand man"); they are joined by a sheriff, the "fiscale" (a Spanish office still retained and primarily involving liaison with the Church); the War Captain (the only civil officer also a religious figure) and his assistants; and a council, usually made up of former governors.

PUEBLO RELIGION AND SOCIETY

Social and religious structure in the pueblos is so complex that what we have put together here is greatly simplified. In most pueblos, society is traditionally made up of two groups, often called the Summer People and the Winter People. The technical anthropological term for these groups is "Moieties." A moiety is simply one of the two factions making up any dual society. Each Pueblo moiety is headed by a chief. The Summer chief is the supreme authority from February to September; the rest of the year the Winter Chief is in command. In effect, during the winter months, the Summer People are subordinate, and vice versa; thus the pattern of traditional Pueblo life follows the course of nature. Serving religious functions under the moiety chiefs are such priestly authorities as the War Captain and his assistants and the heads of the moiety associations.

In some cases, the extremely simplified outline of traditional religious structure presented here is no longer strictly true of the present-day situation. In many pueblos, the old structure has been disturbed by economic and religious problems. At others, native religious ways have vanished almost entirely, sometimes because of acculturation, or because they stopped being passed on from one generation to the next.

In most pueblos, each group has its own kiva, or ceremonial chamber. Sometimes there are three kivas: one for the Winter People, one for the Summer People, and one for ceremonies in which the two groups are ritually united. In some pueblos, Taos for instance, there are multiple kivas. The most recognizable kiva is round, above ground, and unattached to any other building. Examples are found at Cochiti, San Ildefonso, and Santo Domingo. But kivas are also rectangular, and seem to the unfamiliar eye to be nothing more than part of an ordinary row of adobes. Kivas are sacred places and only members of the pueblo are permitted to enter them.

Visitors to the pueblos will find evidence of fusion between native Pueblo religion and Spanish-introduced Catholicism in a few of the ritual dances where a bower protecting a saint's shrine is erected, usually at one end of the dance plaza.

Taos Pueblo Church — Northern

PUEBLO ECONOMY

In times past the pueblo Indians were farmers and hunters. Today they have been gradually forced by social and economic pressures to seek employment away from Pueblo lands, although they do derive income from land leases. Many of the working-age men and women commute to Santa Fe, Albuquerque, or Los Alamos. A major source of Pueblo income is from the production of pottery, jewelry, and other arts and crafts. Ironically, financial problems have played an important role in re-establishing the old crafts; at Nambe, the pottery which was once as fine as Acoma's but fell into a decline, has been revived within the last decade. Much of the fine artistry of the pueblos is represented every day, winter and summer, under the portal of the Palace of the Governors in Santa Fe.

AN IMPORTANT REMINDER

Though tourists are welcome at all of the state's pueblos, there are rules of common courtesy that should be followed. Guidelines include restrictions on photography, sketching, painting and visiting certain areas of the pueblos which are strictly off-limits.

Permits are required for visitors wishing to take photographs or to sketch. Fees for these permits are nominal and vary from pueblo to pueblo. Tape recording is not permitted.

It is advisable to stop at the governor's office of a pueblo before visiting, to ask exactly what is permitted and what is not. The governor's office issues permits and provides information on local recreational facilities open to the public.

PUEBLOS NORTH OF SANTA FE

NAMBE (Nahm-BAY; Tewa for **nambay-ongwee**, "people of the roundish earth"). Located approximately 16 miles north of Santa Fe on I-25, Nambe covers 19,076 acres of land. Its population is approximately 420.

One of the smaller pueblos, Nambe has been continuously occupied since about 1300 A.D. Nambe Indians played an active role in the Pueblo Revolt, murdering their priest and destroying their church. Though the pueblo itself is not spectacular, its prime location is noted for natural beauty and a stunning view of the Sangre de Cristo mountain range. The original village is now completely encircled by non-Indian homes.

Nambe is often considered the most acculturated of the Tewa pueblos; however, a fairly recent renaissance has brought about a renewed interest in traditional rituals and artistry. Nambe Indians today are making a comeback in weaving — particularly cotton belts and kilts — and pottery making. The pottery here is similar to that of Taos and Picuris. Micaceous clay is used to produce both black-on-black and white-on-red styles. Some names to look for are Virginia Gutierrez, Daisy Pena, and Josefita P. Jimenez.

You will want to visit the Nambe Craft Shop, and Nambe Falls, the recreational facility, with fishing and picnicking areas.

PICURIS (Pee-kuhr-REESE; possible Towa origin — **pay kwee layta**, "at mountain gap." The Indians speak Tiwa.) Another of the smaller pueblos with a population of about 198 and an area of 14, 947 acres. Picuris is located about 20 miles south of Taos in the Rio Pueblo Valley just off N.M. 68.

Picuris came into considerable contact with the Plains Indians, as reflected in their dress and ceremonies, and were among the most aggressive of the Pueblo Indians, contributing much to the Revolt, killing their priest and all Spanish in the area.

Visually, Picuris is intriguing because of its unusual puddled adobe construction. Some of these buildings are the oldest of any pueblo along the Rio Grande Valley. The San Lorenzo de Picuris mission exemplifies the melding of Spanish and Indian architecture.

Picuris offers the public an unusually fine museum, picnic area, trout ponds, and archaeological ruins.

Pottery produced at this pueblo is in great demand for its fine quality as cookware. The local micaceous clay is used to produce these pots, which are unpolished and have a golden-brown metallic appearance.

POJOAQUE (Po-WAH-kay; Spanish derivative of Tewa, meaning either "place where the flowers grow along the stream" or "drink water place.") The smallest of the Tewa Pueblos, with 11,601 acres and 130 residents, Pojoaque is located between Nambe and Tesuque.

Pojoaque is historically unique for two reasons. First, it was extinct for several decades. When its already small population was nearly wiped out by the influenza epidemic of 1918 (some villages lost as much as half of their population), the survivors, no longer a self-sustaining entity, moved to other pueblos, many to Santa Clara, some to Nambe. In 1932 the long process of re-establishing Pojoaque began. Fortunately, some of the older structures in the village withstood the passing of time, and there are buildings which date back to well before Coronado. The church, constructed in 1706, is still in use today.

The second unique fact about Pojoaque is that it was the first pueblo to elect a woman as governor, in 1973.

Pojoaque has attracted more industry and business than any other pueblo, and produces income by leasing land to stores, seen from the highway as you approach the turnoff to the village.

Pojoaque pottery, like the village itself, is also making a comeback; it is finely done in the Pueblo tradition, much of it reminiscent of Santa Clara blackware. Lucy Year Flower is perhaps the best known of the potters.

SAN ILDEFONSO (Sahn Eel-day-FAHN-so; Tewa name **pokwo ghay ongwee**, "Place where the water cuts down through"; Spanish named this pueblo for St. Ildephonse, 7th century Archbishop of Toledo.) Visually one of the most beautiful pueblos, San Ildefonso is located 22 miles northwest of Santa Fe (north on I-25 to NM 4 heading west). San Ildefonso is a small pueblo, consisting of about 28,000 acres and some 450 residents. It has achieved national recognition, largely because of its pottery and the friendliness of its people.

It is primarily an agricultural community, although many residents commute to Los Alamos for employment. Of architectural interest is the mission church, which dates back to the 1890's.

This was the home of the late Maria Martinez who, along with her husband Julian, was credited as the source of the renaissance of pueblo arts and crafts which began around the 1920's. Maria developed the famous black matte and highly burnished pottery, a favorite of traders and collectors; her late son, Popovi Da, continued the tradition.

Most contemporary pottery from this pueblo is highly polished blackware with design motifs (often a series of stylized feathers) in a dull, metallic gray, or incised. If incised, the design motif is typically that of the Avanyu, the sacred snake which lives in the clouds and is associated with rain. San Ildefonso blackware can be confused at first with some Santa Clara blackware; the former is usually thinner. San Ildefonso Pueblo also produces polished and decorated redware and polychrome in a tradition usually held to be older than that of the two-tone blackware. Other well-known potters include Santana, Blue Corn, and Rose and Juanita Gonzalez.

You will notice running across the center of the plaza the remnants of the long wall of a houserow. This houserow was tangible evidence of an interesting division of the pueblo, a split between factions which began around 1920. The basis of the split was primarily religious, but family dissensions also entered into the picture. As a result of the dispute, one faction stayed on the north side, nearer Black Mesa (one of the sacred hills), and the other, smaller faction returned to the south side where the round kiva is and has been since sometime in the 14th century. Since the time of separation, San Ildefonso has been constituted by North and South sides instead of by the traditional Winter and

14

Summer moieties.

Two shops are available to the public: the Popovi Da Studio, owned and operated by Mrs. Popovi Da (Anita); and the Alfred Aguilar Studio Shop.

Pottery by
Maria Martinez of
San Ildefonso Pueblo

SAN JUAN (Sahn WAHN; Spanish, "St. John the Baptist.") San Juan is the largest of the Tewa pueblos, with a population of approximately 1700 and 12,238 acres. It is located five miles north of Espanola.

In 1598, the Spanish established the first capital of New Mexico at San Juan, which was then just across the river from its present location, giving the captial the name of San Gabriel but later changing it to San Juan de los Caballeros as tribute to the Indians. Ironically, San Juan was the birthplace of Po-pe, the major force behind the Pueblo Revolt.

Architecturally, San Juan offers the exquisite chapel of Our Lady of Lourdes, dedicated in 1890. The mission is constructed of red volcanic rock.

Offices of the Eight Northern Indian Pueblos Council (ENIPC, the six Tewa Pueblos, plus Taos and Picuris) are located in San Juan. This is a cooperative executive group organized to implement means of improving economic, educational and ceremonial efforts.

Tourists may visit the Oke Oweenge Arts and Crafts Cooperative and the Eight Northern Pueblos Artisans Guild. Acutally, all nineteen pueblos belong to this guild, and arts and crafts from every pueblo are represented here.

Some San Juan names to look for include Bobby Tewa, jeweler; Lorencita Bird, embroidery; Carnation Lockwood, pottery, and Geronima Montoya, painting.

SANTA CLARA (SAHN-tah KLAH-rah; Spanish, St. Clare of Assisi.") Second-largest of the Tewa Pueblos, with a population of more than 1200 and 45,748 acres, Santa Clara is located west of the Rio Grande on N.M. 30 south of Espanola and north of San Ildefonso, with which it shares a common boundary.

The present village site has been occupied for some 400 years. The Santa Clarans trace their ancestry to the Puye settlement cliff-dwelling ruins on the Santa Clara lands, and before that to other ancient sites on the Pajarito Plateau (Pah-hah-REE-to; Spanish, "little bird"). Like other pueblos, Santa Clara joined the Pueblo Revolt. While most of the other pueblos suffered severe punishment at the hands of the Spanish when they reclaimed New Mexico, Santa Clara remained relatively unscathed. However, problems in the late 18th century, such as intertribal warfare over witchcraft and an epidemic, made an impressive dent in the population.

Santa Clara has been the home of noted artist Pablita Velarde. It is also known for its pottery, usually polychrome or highly polished red or blackware, often incised with the ancient symbol of a bear paw.

Names to look for: Van and Lela Gutierrez, potters; Art and Martha Cody, potters; Joseph Lonewolf, potter; and Michael Naranjo, bronze sculpture.

A visitors' center is open to the public; arts, crafts and local foods are available. This pueblo also offers fishing and overnight camping at Santa Clara Canyon. The historic Puye ruins are nearby.

TAOS (rhymes with HOUSE; Spanish derivation of Tewa **tu-o-ta**, "red willow place," or **tua tah**, "down at the village." This is a Tiwa pueblo.) In appearance Taos is probably the most spectacular of the pueblos, distinguished architecturally by its multi-story communal dwellings, forerunners of today's condominiums. It is the northernmost of the Pueblo villages, some 65 miles north of Santa Fe, and about 2 miles north of the town of Taos. Numbering close to 2,000 residents, it contains 95,341 acres. Wheeler Peak, the highest mountain in New Mexico at 13,151 feet, serves as a dramatic backdrop for the pueblo. Taos River cuts through the village, separating North House from South House.

Because it was the northernmost village, Taos was most influenced by the Plains cultures, especially the Kiowa and the Apache, and there is a long tradition of trade between these peoples. The Taos Pueblo owns ample agricultural and grazing lands and good livestock.

Taosenos are noted for a wide variety of crafts, including fine leatherwork, pottery, drums, painting, and quiver-making. Some special names to remember here: Joe Romero, drums; John and Ralph Suazo, stone and wood sculpture, and Quirino Romero, quivermaker.

TESUQUE (Teh-SOO-Kay; Spanish derivation of Tewa **tat'unge'onwi**, "spotted dry place.") Located eight miles north of Santa Fe, and the pueblo closest to the Ancient City, Tesuque has since historic times been the pueblo most in contact with outside cultures. In spite of this, it has remained one of the most traditional of the Tewa villages, and its ceremonials are little changed. The village site has been occupied since 1250 to 1300 A.D. Tesuque lands comprise 16, 813 acres and its inhabitants number approximately 300.

Tesuque played an important role in the Pueblo Revolution; two of its members were inter-pueblo messengers in spreading word of the plot from village to village, and this is where the first blood was shed.

The original church, like churches at many of the pueblos, was destroyed in the revolt. The present one was erected around 1915.

Tesuque women produce a great deal of pottery, mostly in the form of small, brightly painted wares, the lasting effect of suggestions made by an Anglo school teacher back in the 1920's. Since about 1972, however, a few Tesuque potters have returned to the beautiful old kiln-fired pottery. Specialties to look for are the figurines of Manuel Vigil.

THE SOUTHERN AND WESTERN PUEBLOS

ACOMA (AH-ko-mah; Keresan, **ako ma**, "people of the white

rock." Also called the "Sky City.") About 56 miles west of Albuquerque on Interstate 40, this pueblo is the westernmost of the Keresan-speaking pueblos. Its nickname, Sky City, comes from its impressive location on a 357-foot high butte. Acoma has been continuously occupied since 1075 A.D.

Acoma and two outlying areas, Acomita and Santa Maria de Acoma, have about 3200 people who are primarily stockmen and farmers. They raise corn, wheat, melons, squash and hay. Total acreage of the pueblo is 245,672.

Acoma is best-known for its unique polychrome pottery. Traditional designs consist of elaborate geometric elements and burnt-orange and yellow over plain white backgrounds. Acoma pottery was revolutionized in the 1950's by Lucy Lewis, who adapted some Zuni and Mimbres pottery designs to the Pueblo's traditional style. Marie Z. Chino, another well-known potter from Acoma, contributed the use of prehistoric patterns. Descendants of both women still produce pottery today.

Public fishing and picnic facilities are available at nearby Mesa Hill Lake.

COCHITI (KOH-chi-tee; possible Spanish derivation of Tewa Kao Tay-ay, "stone kiva." This is a Keresan-speaking pueblo.) Cochiti is located roughly halfway between Santa Fe and Albuquerque off I-25. Acreage is 28,779 and Cochiti residents number close to 900.

The present site has been occupied since the 13th century, although the Cochitis can trace their ancestral home to the cliff dwellings at Bandelier. The so-called "Stone Lions," replicas of which are on view not far from the museum at Bandelier, were once part of a sacred kiva-type edifice in the hills, the object of Cochiti pilgrimages for hunting rituals even now.

Formerly an agricultural community, some residents still work the land while others commute to Albuquerque and Santa Fe for work.

Cochiti is noted for its drums — particularly double-headed aspen or cottonwood drums — and jewelry. There has been a resurgence in production of pottery, characterized by a creamy white slip, and designs painted in black with animal forms. The famous "Storyteller," a maternal figure surrounded by children, is a popular innovation created by Mrs. Helen Cordero in the early 1970's.

The Spanish mission built in the early 17th century still stands. In use today, the mission is named San Buenaventura de Cochiti.

Cochiti's once-quiet existence has been broken by the construction of Cochiti Dam, a five-mile-long earthfill dam forming a lake used for irrigation and recreation. Boaters, picnickers and fishermen will find this a delightful facility.

Black Mesa near San Ildefonso Pueblo
and sacred to all Northern Pueblos

ISLETA (Ees-LEH-tah; Spanish, "little island." Isleta is located thirteen miles south of Albuquerque on U.S. 85. An agricultural community, Isleta is the largest of the Tiwa-speaking Pueblos with close to 3,000 residents and 210,948 acres.

It has occupied the same site since before Coronado appeared in 1540 and served as a way station for every Spanish explorer passing through New Mexico. The only pueblo which did not participate in the Pueblo Revolt, Isleta instead joined the Spanish on their retreat to El Paso del Norte.

Many of the Indians left the pueblo and moved to Hopi land during those troublesome times. When friction ceased, they moved back, bringing with them Hopi mates and Hopi-Tiwa children. In the late 1800's certain members of Laguna and Acoma also emigrated to Isleta. This led to internal disagreements over religion and the emigrants eventually banded together to establish Oraibi. Today, Isleta is comprised of the main settlement and the two smaller colonies, Chicale and Oraibi. The mission, San Agustin de Isleta, was built in 1709.

Shadow
of cross and
gate at entrance to
Picuris Pueblo
Church — Northern

Isletans depend for their livelihood primarily on jobs at nearby military bases, with businesses in nearby Albuquerque, or with the Bureau of Indian Affairs.

Pottery is produced, although much of it until the 1970's was made purely for tourists and had little traditional value. One family, however, Chiwiwi, has returned to traditional style pottery production, combining Isleta and Laguna elements of design. Isletans are also acclaimed for their highly popular breads. Look for jewelry by Ted Charveze, embroidery by Jesse Overstreet, and pottery by Stella Teller.

Fishing and camping facilities are available at Sunrise Lake.

JEMEZ (HAY-mess; Tanoan, **hay-mish**, "people.") Located about 20 miles northwest of Bernalillo on N.M. 63, just off U.S. 85, Jemez numbers over 1900 residents and has 88,867 acres.

Jemez is the last remaining Towa-speaking pueblo; among its residents are descendants of Pecos Pueblo, also Towa, the last seventeen residents of which were removed to Jemez in 1838. The present Jemez site has been occupied since sometime during the 16th century, although the actual pueblo was not constructed until after the Pueblo Revolt.

Jemez women still weave yucca baskets, a lost art among other Pueblos, and garments — some ceremonial as well as other items such as belts — which are for sale. Jemez women are prolific potters. Some produce beautiful work in the traditional style, but many create pots primarily for tourist consumption. The latter are decorated in glossy black and brown designs, somewhat similar in effect to the pottery of Tesuque. A well-known Jemez artist is Mrs. Lucy Yepa Lowden, known in particular for her life-like Indian figures, but also a skilled weaver and potter.

LAGUNA (Lah GOO-nah; Spanish, "lake." Largest of the Keresan-speaking Pueblos, Laguna is located 40 miles west of Albuquerque on I-40. Laguna and its satellite communities share 742,315 acres. Population of the area is close to 6,000.

Lagunans are of mixed origin, including Tanoan, Keresan, Shoshone, and Zuni. Archaeologists estimate that settlement of the pueblo dates from 1450. The mission, San Jose de Laguna, dates from 1699 and is notable for its decoration.

A progressive pueblo, Laguna has traditionally earned its livelihood from grazing livestock. The land is situated on one of the richest uranium fields in the world and many of the Indians are miners.

21

Pottery-making had been abandoned at Laguna until the early 1970's when a conservation and education program, funded by Manpower Development and Training Act, reestablished the art form. Traditional Laguna pottery was very similar to that of Acoma, with its geometric designs and red, orange, and yellow accents. Laguna artists include: Bruce Lubo, painter; Christopher Luther, painter; Duane Mabtia, contemporary jeweler and painter; Alan C. Nateway, jeweler; Josephita Jeremiah, potter; Evelyn Jeremiah, potter.
Paguate Reservoir is open to public fishing.

SANDIA (Sahn-DEE-ah; Tiwa, **nafiat**, "dusty or sandy.") With a population of about 300 and 22,884 acres, Sandia is located just off I-25, 14 miles north of Albuquerque. The pueblo seen today was founded in 1742. The orginal pueblo was abandoned by its inhabitants, who fled to Hopi land during the Pueblo Revolt.
Most Sandians derive their incomes from corporate, government, or industrial jobs. A few are farmers and cattle ranchers.
Virgina Naranjo is a well-known Sandia storyteller. However, the pueblo is very conservative and permits no drawing, painting or photography.

SAN FELIPE (Sahn Fay-LEE-pay; Spanish, "St. Philip.") This 18th century Keres pueblo is located about 30 miles north of Albuquerque. Like its neighbor, Santo Domingo, it is conservative to the point of regarding visitors as intruders. Because of this, San Felipe has retained much of its Indian heritage.
Approximately 1850 people live at San Felipe; many of the adult males are farmers, but a high percentage work in nearby Albuquerque. A unique physical feature of the village is the sunken plaza, about three feet below the level of the surrounding houses, which provides a specially beautiful setting for ceremonial dances. Another interesting feature is the San Felipe church, an excellent example of early Franciscan mission architecture.

SANTA ANA (SAHN-tah AH-nah; Spanish, "St. Anne." Keresan.) Located approximately 8 miles northwest of Bernalillo on the banks of the Jemez River, Santa Ana is a "recent" pueblo, probably founded around the turn of the 18th century after the reconquest of the Spaniards in 1692-1694. The location of the original pueblo site is unknown. Like most of the down-river pueblos, it is extremely conservative.
Because its land for the most part is too barren for farming,

many of its residents (around 500; 44,489 acres) have moved away, either to jobs or to more productive farm land, returning to the village only for religious ceremonies. Crafts have nonetheless remained an important aspect of community life. Red textile belts and headbands are still woven here, mostly for ceremonial use. Until 1973 only one woman was making pottery, but she has since trained a number of village women, and today there are quite a few excellent potters.

Santa Ana has a sales outlet, formed by the Ta-ma-myia Cooperative Assocation, which sells pottery, jewelry, textiles and foods.

Taos Pueblo
— detail —
adobe walled
entrance to church proper

SANTO DOMINGO (SAHN-toh Do-MEEN-goh; Spanish, "St. Dominic.") This is the most conservative of all the pueblos, and is the largest of the Keresan group with 74,190 acres and a population of about 2500.

The pueblo took a particularly active role in the Pueblo Revolt, although it soon after abandoned its village and relocated in the Jemez Mountains. Santo Domingo was among the last of the pueblos to surrender to DeVargas, after which they returned to their former village. A portion of the village was built in 1692, though much of what is seen today was built after 1886, the year in which a flood washed away the old buildings.

Santo Domingo is noted for the quality of its silver-work and for hishi (also spelled heishi, pronounced HEE-she), bits of shell rolled by hand into tiny round beads which are then hand-drilled and strung. Pottery is similar to that of Cochiti — the same creamy white slip is used; however, the designs are different. The highly conservative nature of the Pueblo precludes innovations, such as Mrs. Cordero's "Storyteller" at Cochiti, and there is more demonstration of skill in decoration, firing, form, and thinness of wall.

ZIA (ZEE-ah, Keres, **tsia**). This Keresan-speaking Pueblo is 16 miles northwest of Bernalillo and is the source of the familiar sun symbol used on the New Mexico State flag, license plates, and elsewhere.

Zia suffered severely in the aftermath of the Pueblo Revolt. Nearly 600 people were killed and continued wars and pestilence greatly reduced its population. Today the pueblo has about 800 residents and 112,510 acres. The land is poor and has limited irrigation water, yet agriculture is the mainstay of the economy. A prominent feature of the Pueblo's appearance is corrals for livestock. Another feature is the mission, which dates from 1692.

Zia potters are among the most skillful of Pueblo artists, resisting innovations in design and form, and adhering strictly to Zia tradition. A familiar design motif is the turkey. Zia pots are typically unpolished redware over which a white slip has been partly laid. Designs are painted in brown or a muted black.

ZUNI (ZOON-yee; Keresan, **sunyi'tsi**.) Forty miles south of Gallup on N.M. 53, this pueblo was the first to be seen by Europeans, but it has successfully managed to resist most outside influences.

This pueblo rivals Laguna in both population — close to 7,000 — and in size — 408,404 acres.

The Zuni Indians are farmers and are widely acclaimed for their fine inlaid jewelry. Pottery and weaving are produced in limted amounts. Several years ago, Daisy Hooie, descendant of Nampeyo, famous Hopi potter, began working with the Zuni women in order to help them redevelop their pottery making skills.

Sha'lak'o, (Sha-lak-o) most famous of all New Mexico ceremonial dances, is held at Zuni each December. The murals of Alex Seotewa at Nuestra Senora de Guadalupe Mission Church are another attraction.

Northern Pueblo man

Detail of an adobe brick passageway,
Old Pecos Monument near Pecos, New Mexico

BIBLIOGRAPHY

Brody, J.D. **Indian Painters and White Patrons.** Albuquerque: University of New Mexico Press, 1971.

Dozier, Edward P. **The Pueblo Indians of North America.** Holt, Rinehart, and Winston, Inc., 1970. Available in paperback.

Dutton, Bertha. **Indians of New Mexico.** Commerce and Industry Department, Tourism Division, 1975. (pamphlet)

Folsom, Franklin. **Red Power on the Rio Grande: The Native American Revolution of 1680.** Follett Publishing Company, 1973. Also suitable for children.

Handbook of North American Indians, Vol. 9, Alfonso Ortiz, editor. Washington, D.C.: Smithsonian Institution, 1979. See entries on specific pueblos.

Hightower, Jamake. **Ritual of the Wind: North American Indian Ceremonies, Music and Dances.** New York: Viking Press, 1977.

Marriott, Alice. **Maria, The Potter of San Ildefonso.** University of Oklahoma Press, 1948. The biography of Maria Martinez in novel form.

Lange, Charles, H. **Cochiti: A New Mexico Pueblo, Past and Present.** University of Texas Press, 1959. Available in paperback.

LeFree, Betty. **Santa Clara Pottery Today.** Albuquerque: University of New Mexico Press, 1975.

Maxwell Museum of Anthropology. **Seven Families in Pueblo Pottery.** Albuquerque: University of New Mexico Press, 1974.

New Perspectives on the Pueblos. Alfonso Ortiz, editor. University of New Mexico Press, 1972.

Ortiz, Alfonso. **The Tewa World.** University of Chicago Press, 1969. A comprehensive and scholarly but highly readable treatment of Tewa thought and socio-religious structure.

Sando, Joe. **The Pueblo Indians.** San Francisco: Indian Historic Press, 1976.

Spinden, Herbert J. **Songs of the Tewa.** The Exposition of Indian Tribal Arts, Inc., 1933. Published in a new edition by The Sunstone Press, 1975. Sacred and secular song-poems of the Tewa in Dr. Spinden's sensitive translations, with introductory essay.

Toulouse, Betty. **Pueblo Pottery of the New Mexico Indians: Ever Constant, Ever Changing.** Santa Fe: Museum of New Mexico Press, 1977.

Van Etten, Teresa. **Ways of Indian Magic.** Santa Fe: Sunstone Press, 1984.

Whitman, William. **The Pueblo of San Ildefonso.** Columbia University Press. Contributions to Anthropology No. 34, 1947. Out of print but available in Santa Fe Public and museum libraries. The library of the Laboratory of Anthropology is open to the public.

Ladder entrance to the cliff dwelling,
Bandelier National Monument

FIESTAS, DANCES AND CEREMONIES

January 1 — New Year Celebration — Taos, Santo Domingo, San Felipe, Cochiti, Santa Ana, Picuris; Turtle, corn and various other dances.

January 6 — King's Day and Installation of new officials — Santo Domingo, San Felipe, Cochiti, Santa Clara, Santa Ana, Taos, Picuris; Eagle, Elk, Buffalo, Deer Dance.

Date set each year — Election celebration (3 weeks after election on January 6) San Juan; Basket, Cloud, Deer Dance.

January 23 — Feast Day — San Ildefonso; Buffalo and Deer Dance (North Side) Commanche Dance (South Side).

January 25 — Picuris

February 1st week — Governor's Feast — Acoma; various dances.

February 2 — Candelaria Day Celebration — San Felipe, Santo Domingo, Picuris; Buffalo and various other dances.

Date set each year — San Juan, Santa Clara; Deer Dance and Buffalo Dance.

Date set each year — Isleta; Evergreen Dance.

March 19 — St. Joseph's Feast — Laguna; Harvest and Social Dance.

Easter — Spring Corn Dance, Basket and various dances — San Ildefonso, San Felipe, Santa Ana, Santo Domingo, Santa Clara, Cochiti.

May 1 — Feast Day — San Felipe (St. Philip); Green Corn Dance.

May 3 — Santa Cruz Day — Taos; Green Corn Dance and Children's races.

May 3 — Santa Cruz Day and coming of the Rivermen — Cochiti.

Date set each year — Blessing of the fields — Tesuque; Corn or Flag Dance.

June 13 — St. Anthony's Feast Day — Sandia, San Ildefonso, San Juan, Taos, Picuris; Corn Dance.

June 13 — St. Anthony's Feast Day — Santa Clara; Commanche and various dances.

June 23-24 — St. John the Baptist Feast Day — San Juan; Vespers, Buffalo Dance on evening of 23rd, War Dances and foot races on 24th.

June 24 — St. John the Baptist Feast Day — Taos; Corn Dance.

June 24 — St. John the Baptist Feast day — Cochiti; Grab Day.
June 29 — San Pedro's Day — Rooster Pulls at Acoma; Corn Dance at San Felipe, Santa Ana, Santo Domingo.
July 4 — Nambe; various dances.
July 14 — St. Bonaventure's Feast Day — Cochiti; Corn Dance.
July 25 — Celebration of St. James — San Felipe, Acoma, Cochiti, Laguna, Santo Domingo; Grab Day; Taos — Corn Dance.
July 26 — St. Anne's Day — Santa Ana, Taos; Corn Dance.
Date set each year — Santa Clara; Puye Cliff Ceremonial.
August 2 — Jemez; Old Pecos Bull Dance.
August 4 — St Dominic's Day — Santo Domingo; Corn Dance.
August 9-10 — St. Lawrence Day — Picuris; Sunset Dance on 9th, dances and foot races on 10th.
August 10 — St. Lawrence Day — Acoma; Corn Dance.
August 10 — St. Lawrence Day — Cochiti, Laguna; Grab Day.
August 12 — St. Clare's Feast Day — Santa Clara.
August 15 — Our Lady of Assumption Feast Day — Zia; Corn Dance.
August 15 — Feast of St. Anthony — Laguna; Harvest and Social Dances.
August 28 — Isleta; Spanish fiesta.

September 2 — St. Stephen's Feast Day — Acoma.
September 4 — St. Augustine's Feast Day — Isleta.
September 8 — Laguna; Harvest and Social Dance.
September 8 — San Ildefonso; Corn Dance.
Date set for last week of the month — San Juan; Harvest Dance.
September 14-15 — Jicarilla Apache; Jicarilla Fair-rodeos, pow wows, foot races, dances.
September 19 — St. Joseph's Feast Day — Laguna; Harvest Dance.
September 25 — St. Elizabeth's Feast Day — Laguna; Harvest and Social Dance.
September 29-30 — San Geronimo's Feast Day — Taos; Sundown Dance on evening of 29th. War and various types of dances, trade fair, races and pole climbing on the 30th.

October 4 — San Francisco de Assisi Feast Day — Nambe; Elk and various dances.
October 17 — St. Margaret's Day — Laguna; Harvest and Social Dance.

November 12 — San Diego's Feast Day — Jemez, Corn Dance; Tesuque, Flag, Buffalo, Deer or Commanche Dance.

December — Date set each year — Zuni; Sha'lak'o Dance.
December 12 — Celebration of Our Lady of Guadalupe — Jemez, Matachines; Pojoaque, Commanche or Buffalo and Bow and Arrow Dances.
December 24-25 — Christmas Celebration — San Juan, Matachines, religious procession; Taos, Deer Dance or Matachines Dance and torchlight procession.

December 25 — Christmas Celebration — Picuris, San Ildefonso, Santa Clara, Tesuque; Matachines Dance.

December 25 — Christmas Celebration — Jemez, Santa Ana, San Felipe, Santo Domingo, Cochiti; Buffalo, Deer, Harvest, Basket, Rainbow, Matachines and various other dances.

December 26 — San Juan; Turtle Dance.

Most festivities begin mid-morning and continue until sunset.

**Stormy view of Old Pecos Monument
taken during restoration**

INDEX

Acoma Pueblo, 8, 12, 17-18
Acomita, 18
Aguilar, Alfred, 15
Bandelier National Monument,
  8, 18
Bird, Lorencita, 16
Blue Corn (potter), 14
Charveze, Ted, 21
Chino, Maria Z., 18
Cochiti Pueblo, 8, 18-19
Cody, Art, 16
Cody, Martha, 16
Cordero, Helen, 18, 24
Coronado, Francisco Vasquez de,
  13, 19-20
Da, Anita, 15
Da, Popovi, 14
De Vargas, Don Diego SEE
  Vargas, Don Diego de
Eight Northern Indian Pueblos
  Council (ENIPC), 15-16
Flower, Lucy Year, 14
Gonzales, Jose, 9
Gonzalez, Juanita, 14
Gonzalez, Rose, 14
Gutierrez, Lela, 16
Gutierrez, Van, 16
Gutierrez, Virginia, 12
Hooie, Daisy, 24
Isleta Pueblo, 8, 19-21
Jemez Pueblo, 8, 21
Jeremiah, Evelyn, 22
Jeremiah, Josephita, 22
Jimenez, Josefita P., 12
Kivas, 10-11
Laguna Pueblo, 8, 21-22, 24
Lewis, Lucy, 18
Lockwood, Carnation, 16
Lonewolf, Joseph, 16
Lowden, Lucy Yepa, 21
Lubo, Bruce, 22
Luther, Christopher, 22
Mabita, Duane, 22
Manpower Development and
  Training Act, 22
Martinez, Julian, 14
Martinez, Maria, 14
Mogollon, Juan Ignacio Flores, 7
Montoya, Geronima, 16
Nambe Pueblo, 7-8, 12-13
Naranjo, Michael, 16
Narnajo, Virginia, 22
Nateway, Alan C., 22

Nuestra Senora de Guadalupe
  Mission, 25
Oraibi, 20
Our Lady of Lourdes Chapel, 15
Overstreet, Jesse, 21
Pecos Pueblo, 21
Pena, Daisy, 12
Perez, Albino, 9
Picuris Pueblo, 7-8, 12-13
Pope, 9, 15
Pueblo Revolt of 1680, 9, 12-13,
  15-17, 20-24
Pueblo Revolt of 1837, 9
Pueblo Revolt of 1847, 9
Pojoaque Pueblo, 7-8, 13-14
Pueblos; Economy, 11-12
  Government, 10
  History, 8-9
  Language, 8
  Religion, 10-11
Puye Ruins, 16
Romero, Joe, 17
Romero, Quirino, 17
San Augustin de Isleta Mission, 20
San Buenaventura de Cochiti
  Mission, 18
San Felipe Pueblo, 8, 22
San Gabriel SEE
  San Juan
San Ildefonso Pueblo, 7-8, 14-15
San Jose de Laguna Mission, 21
San Juan Pueblo, 7-8, 15-16
San Lorenzo de Picuris Mission, 13
Sandia Pueblo, 8, 22
Santa Ana Pueblo, 8, 22-23
Santa Clara Pueblo, 7-8, 13-14, 16
Santa Maria de Acoma, 18
Santana (potter), 14
Santo Domingo Pueblo, 8, 22-24
Seotewa, Alex, 25
Suazo, John, 17
Suazo, Ralph, 17
Taos Pueblo, 7-8, 12, 16-17
Teller, Stella, 21
Tesuque Pueblo, 7-8, 13, 17
Tewa, Bobby, 16
Towa, 21
Tsankawi, 8
Vargas, Don Diego de, 9, 24
Velarde, Pablita, 16
Vigil, Manuel, 17
Zia Pueblo, 8, 24
Zuni Pueblo, 8, 24-25